Beware of the Teenager!

Jokes of sympathy
for surviving parents

By PAM BROWN

with cartoons by
DOMINIC POELSMA

EXLEY

© Pam Brown (text)
© Dominic Poelsma (illustrations)

First published 1986 by Exley Publications Ltd,
16 Chalk Hill, Watford WD1 4BN.

Printed and bound in Great Britain by
Hazell, Watson & Viney Ltd.

Brown, Pam
Beware of the teenager!
1. Youth — Anecdotes, facetiae, satire, etc. I. Title
305.2'35'0207 HQ793

ISBN 1-85015-052-5

Preface

Pick up any history and there they are, the Terrible Young who were all set to destroy civilisation: whooping it up in Greece or Rome, in Elizabethan England, in the pages of Edwardian novels... given to outlandish fashions and raucous parties, rude to their elders, rebellious, shiftless and alarming. Remember the terrible Lupin. ... cutting up the other traffic on the road ... behind a horse, rather than behind a souped-up engine? Perhaps it is time we stopped sticking labels on the young. On *anyone* for that matter. The Teens was a phenomenon invented by manufacturers who had sniffed out a huge new market. There *are* no standard Teenagers: just a generation of young people trying, as young people have done since the age of the cave, to bridge the chasm between childhood and adult responsibility, hating the mess the previous generations have bequeathed them, and wondering how in hell they are to put it right.

Time will pass. Their own teenagers are waiting for them just over the horizon.

So, forgive us. One day you will know for yourselves that parents have terrible difficulty in coming to terms with the fact that the baby they longed for, the child they played with and whose future they dreamed about, has gone and grown up. How on earth can mothers and fathers reconcile this huge young man with an incipient beard with the little lad whose teddy bear still sits on the chest of drawers: this self-assured young woman with the little girl doggedly practising the Brownie Law. Especially as they are never the same people for three weeks together, being occupied by trying out permutations of personality.

Be patient with us. The dust does settle.

PAM BROWN

Teenagers smile secret smug smiles in public places.

"That you, mother? I just fancied a cup of coffee."

The problem starts when you're not sure whether it is
your son or daughter. . .

The books warn you that teenagers will be moody.
They just don't say HOW moody.

No teenager is the shape it would like to be.

Teenagers don't like parents to get trendy.

If you listen very quietly you will hear your six foot macho son asking the cat if "sweetie's got a poor little sore foot."

Teenagers: have a brilliant academic career ahead of them.

Adults: have a brilliant career behind them.

Teenagers: think a lot about the meaning of life.

Adults: mean to when they get a minute to themselves.

Teenagers: look forward to having a baby. . .

Adults: know babies turn into teenagers.

Teenagers are divided into: Look at me's and...

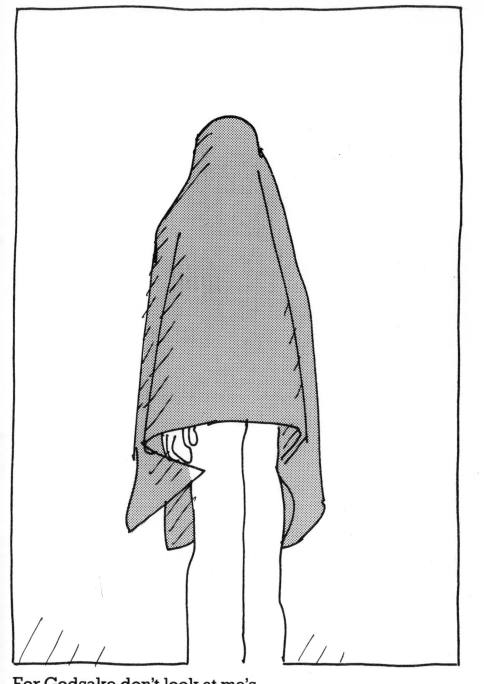

For Godsake don't look at me's.

"She explained it to me – This generation NEEDS marijuana to relax them under the pressure of modern living. . ."

"All I ask is to be left alone!" (So long as you do the washing, ironing, cook her meals and let her play her stereo as loud as she likes.)

"Ma and Pa are parents, not people!"

"No, she's eighteen actually."

The teens is the time when you find a mother can't always kiss it better.

"She must be home – it's today's newspaper."

When your teenage daughter lets you hold her hand,
she's in REAL trouble.

There is nothing that terrifies the clergy more than the teenager who has found God.

A teenager is always playing to an invisible gallery.

For every half a dozen teenagers trying to show off their bumps there are hundreds frantically trying to flatten them.

Bumps.

The teens is when your brain is at its best – but you don't feel like using it.

A teenager is that baby you yearned for.

Nothing embarrasses a teenager as much as an adult trying to relate to him.

"Mother! What a silly hair-cut!"

When you welcome your teenager home from three weeks' hiking, you welcome home. . .

three weeks laundry.

If he likes the tape, the entire road gets the tape.

"But Mom, how do you FEEL about exploitation?"

The teenager who won't go out of the house with a crease in her blouse, is the one with the cultivated patch across the behind of her jeans.

Teenagers genuinely can't understand adults' low noise tolerance.

Every generation has to have a swear word that will
unnerve the PREVIOUS generation.

"Is that it?"

Teenagers bank on the fact that you won't ACTUALLY kill them.

Teenage sex is lying awake thinking what an IDIOT you made of yourself.

It is almost impossible to tell whether an inarticulate
teenager is shy, stupid or "cool".

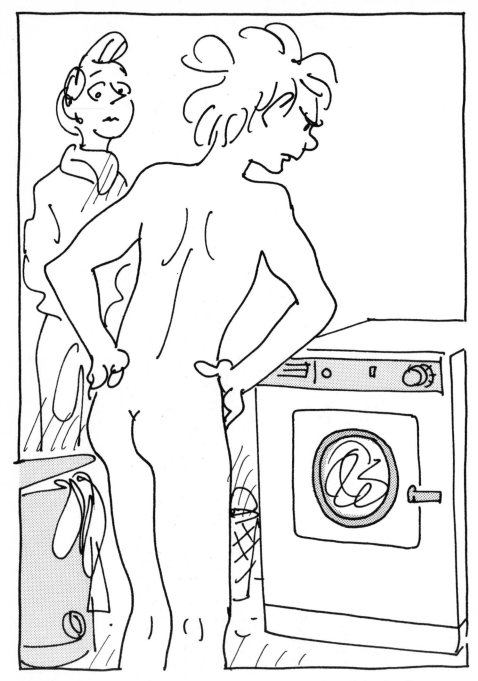

The only shirt your teenager wants is the shirt in the wash.

"Mom! Your bloody hair spray's running out!"

A teenager is a creature whose existence is only
proved to the family by the chaos in her room, floods
in the bathroom and the empty refrigerator.

"No she's not actually pregnant – just pessimistic."

Those old jeans you threw out took her months to get exactly that way.

"I know there are compensations. It's just that I can't think of any."

"Well, this one is CLEAN. . ."

The family is about give and take.
Parents give – Teenagers take.

Teenagers who lock themselves in the bathroom are
more likely to be applying face packs than smoking pot.

A lump in her bed at eleven in the morning is routine.
A lump in her bed during "Cagney & Lacey" means an
ambulance call.

"Fancy suggesting that I should give Teddy to The Salvation Army."

A teenager knows no-one has ever felt like this before.

Teenagers are horribly shocked and hurt when they succeed in driving their parents into a towering rage.

Every generation of teenagers thinks it's discovered the ultimate in style. The trouble being the photographs – twenty years on.

The strange strangled noise in the back of your
teenager's throat is him saying, "Thank you".

Every teenager knows she is going to be famous.

Other gift books from Exley Publications

Grandmas and Grandpas, £4.50. $7.95. Children are close to grandparents, and this book of children's sayings reflects that warmth. "Your grandma loves you, no matter what you do", "A grandma is old on the outside but young on the inside"; "A grandma is jolly and when she laughs a warmness spreads over you. This is a very, very popular book, which makes a particularly loving present for grandparents.
To Dad, £4.50, $7.95. "Fathers are always right, and even if they're not right, they're never actually wrong". Dads will love this book — it's so true to life!
To Mom, £4.50. $7.95. "When I'm sad she patches me up with laughter." A thoughtful, joyous gift for Mom entirely created by children. Get it for Mother's Day or her birthday.
For Mother, a gift of love, £4.95. $7.95. Poets and writers old and new, from Ogden Nash to Noël Coward, from C. Day Lewis to D. H. Lawrence, from Margaret Mead to Rudyard Kipling, reflect on their mothers in this thoughtful collection. The book is sensitively illustrated with fine grey-screened photographs and paintings by people like Van Gogh and Picasso which match the moods of the writers.
Marriage, a keepsake, £4.95. $7.95. In the same series, but with a dove-grey suedel cover. This collection of poems and prose celebrates marriage with some of the finest love messages between husbands and wives. A gift for all ages — from those about to be married to those who have known fifty good years and more together.

United Kingdom
Free catalogue available on request. Books may be ordered through your bookshop, or by post from Exley Publications, Dept. TD, 16 Chalk Hill, Watford, Herts, United Kingdom WD1 4BN. Please add 95p as a contribution to postage and packing.